About The Book

Laura Hillenbrand's second full-length focuses on the life of Louis Zamperini, the Olympic miler who became a war hero. His story has the ring of an Errol Flynn adventure flick (although Basil Rathbone would have made a bad Mutsuhiro Watanabe), and ever since his return home people have been vying for the rights to his story.

Zamperini has twice released his own version of the events, both under the title *The Devil at my Heels.* This work, along with the two original accounts, represents a precious resource in the field of history. It is important for these stories to be told; as our World War Two veterans are approaching old age, we need to record their stories and document their journeys just as Hillenbrand has done here. It is important to study the hard facts of war, but we also need to try and come to terms with the emotional and very personal thing that a war is for the people who experience it. In volunteering at the Windsor Historical Society's <u>Veterans' Memories Project</u>, I have come to understand the historical value of the veteran's experience.

The internet has been filled with possible film rumors since the book was released in 2010. It is unclear whether this is a reflection of the power of Louie's story, or a belief that everything Hillenbrand writes is going to be made into a movie. The <u>movie</u> version is apparently set to be released in 2013 by Universal Studios. No matter the medium, Zamperini's story is an amazing adventure and is sure to move audiences.

About The Author

Laura Hillenbrand was born in Fairfax Virginia on May 15, 1967. She is a journalist and writer, and won the William Hill Sports Book of the Year in 2001 for her first book, *Seabiscuit: An American Legend*, which was shortlisted for many other awards and won the Book Sense Book of the Year. While some reviewers have dedicated space to comparing the two works, it is sufficient to say that both books are thought-provoking and emotionally charged. They deal with completely separate topics, but both books put on full display the dazzling story-telling of Ms. Hillenbrand.

Many magazines have had the honor of publishing Hillenbrand's work, including *Equus Magazine, The New Yorker,* and *American Heritage*. In 1998, she won the Eclipse Award for Magazine Writing. Hillenbrand has written on a wide range of topics including horses, history, and her personal battle with disease.

Among her many passions, Hillenbrand is a dedicated philanthropist and the co-founder of Operation International Children, which started in 2003 as Operation Iraqi Children. The foundation coordinates its efforts with American soldiers to provide children in poverty-stricken areas with school supplies, toys, blankets, and clothes.

Hillenbrand rarely leaves her Washington D.C. home because she suffers from Chronic Fatigue Syndrome. The debilitating disorder has plagued the author since her college days. Hillenbrand transcends her physical limitations vicariously through the lives of her chosen subjects. While reading through *Unbroken,* this passion is almost radiating through the pages.

Overall Summary

<u>Louis Silvie Zamperini</u> was born on January 26, 1917 in Olean, New York. His parents, Anthony and Louise, had immigrated from Italy only a few years previously. From the time he was born, the little boy that they called "toots" was a handful. The family moved to Torrance, California because of Louie's pneumonia and they were one of the few Italian families in the area.

With a natural desire to challenge authority, Louis grew to be a master thief and trouble maker. When the police in Torrance received a call, his door was the first they knocked at. His life was headed to the gutter when his brother Pete started coaching Louis as a runner.

Louis broke high school and college track records before he qualified for the 1936 Berlin Olympics. His race impressed many as he ran the fastest lap in the 5000 meters, but he ran it too late and finished 7th. The feat "earned" Louie a handshake from Hitler, and the admiration of his countrymen. He returned to the United States and continued to set UCAA records and he was focused on winning at the next Olympic games.

When the Second World War broke out, Louie joined the Air Force and started training as a Bombardier. He flew in B-24s and completed several combat missions before his plane went down, due to engine failure, in the middle of the Pacific. After 47 days at sea surviving on raw albatross, terns, pilot fish, and shark liver, and having rain as the only source of drinking water, Louie arrived in the Marshall Islands and was turned over to the Japanese prison camps.

A demented Corporal named "The Bird" had taken over Omori prison camp as he was so cruel that the guards and officers defer to him. The Bird had taken a special interest in officers who were successful in civilian life and especially those who do not submit to his authority. Louie was beaten daily by Watanabe and the image of the man was imprinted on the psyche of the runner. As the war ends, Watanabe is on the run as a wanted war criminal and Louie is received as a hero.

Through the late 1940s Zamperini lived in California, but had never been able to leave the camps behind. Louie, like the vast majority of the Pacific POWs, suffered from the psychological torture he endured. It was not until he heard Billy Graham that Louie remembered the promise he had made so many times during his time on the raft and in the camps: to dedicate his life to God. In 1954, Louis opened Victory Boys Camp, a center for troubled boys. Over the years, he has tried to keep his promise to God through his camp and his public speaking. Louie Zamperini forgave all of the Japanese guards.

Chapter-By-Chapter Summaries

Part One

The One-Boy Insurgency

The story begins in 1929 with the *Graf Zeppelin* passing over Torrance, California on its way to circumnavigating the globe, a moment that Zamperini remembered vividly from his childhood. The family had moved to Torrance in 1919 because of two-year-old Louie's bout with pneumonia. The town was not excited to welcome Italians into its city limits and the Zamperini's had to deal with the prejudices of the small community.

Eventually, they are able to move into a proper house, but the young immigrant family starts out in a one room shack built with their own hands. Mrs. Zamperini takes to guarding her small property with a rolling pin, ready to take on all intruders. Louis has to deal with the stigma associated with both his ethnicity and his class.

Often seen running through the back alleys of Torrance, Louis was a known thief and rabble-rouser. When things went missing in Torrance people knew whose door to knock on. Louis had also learned that if adults saw two boys fighting they would give them quarters to stop and so he started fights all over town to make money.

Louis was tormented by bullies until his father taught him how to box and made Louis a makeshift set of exercise equipment out of tin cans and pipes. Louis, no longer afraid, began to terrorize the streets of Torrance. His parents had no idea how they were going to deal with Louis because the police were constantly at their door, the neighbours were always complaining, and no amount of punishment seemed to change Louie's behaviour.

As Louie enters high school, he begins to realize that he needs to change. One factor that Hillenbrand points to is California's fascination with eugenics. As Louis enters his teens a troublesome young man, his home state becomes enrapt in an effort to dispose of undesirables through chemical castration and incarceration. There were probably a host of reasons for Louie's attempts to quit stealing, drinking, and fighting, but this was a big worry for California's juvenile delinquents of the 1930s.

Run Like Mad

In 1931, Louie learned that any key had a 1-in-50 chance of working, which was how he gained access to the Torrance High School Gym, and this was the beginning of a basketball ticket scam. School authorities began to notice a lot more students with tickets than their ledger could account for. This little stunt and the backlash from authorities was what prompted Pete Zamperini to stand up for his younger brother and coach the troubled youngster in track and field.

While Louis was a terrible runner in his first year on the track, Pete did not give up. Pete used to ride his bicycle behind his younger brother and whack him with a stick if he ran too slowly. The training paid off and that year he became the first Torrance student to compete in the all-city finals.

Louie's rebellious side had yet to die out and after a spat with his father he ran away from home. Joining up with some friends the boys decided to jump on a train to leave Torrance behind. The misadventure ends with the boys jumping from a moving train to escape under the watchful eye of a railroad detective with an un-holstered gun. Louis returned home hungry and humbled.

Louie's track performance was astounding, and in 1933, at the age of 16, he began competing against college students, winning the UCLA meets at both the mile and two-mile distances. His social life had improved as well. The once-outcast was elected class president and was attending many parties.

The Torrance Tornado

At the Southern California Track and field Championship in 1934, Louie surpasses expectations and sets a new record for high school milers, running the race in a blistering 4:21.3. The town that had once shunned him now embraces their track star. The hometown papers dub Zamperini "the Torrance Tornado" and Louie begins to think about the possibility of competing in the upcoming Olympics in Berlin.

As one of the younger runners who would be competing for a spot on the US Olympic team, Louie elects to try for the much longer 5000m race. The distance is gruelling but the field of competitors is not as deep and Louie believes he has a good shot to earn a spot on the team. On July 3, 1936, a huge crowd gathers to see Louie's train leave for New York. He spends his travel time flirting with every young woman on the train.

Don Lash, three time NCAA champion in the 5000m, was also running for a spot in Berlin, but

Louie knew he just needed to come in third in the final race. Louie waited back in the pack through the many laps of the distance event, when Lash tried to rest before the final push, Louie started his final kick and blasted past the race leaders. Lash took off after the young upstart and hunted him down catching Zamperini at the tape, but even the announcer did not know. Race fans back in Torrance were elated by the erroneous proclamation of Zamperini's victory. Louis Zamperini was now an Olympian.

Plundering Germany

Transatlantic travel was still mainly an aquatic adventure in 1936 and so the American Olympians were loaded onto the *Manhattan*, a luxury steamer. With the athletes fighting for space, the availability of large quantities of rich foods, and the swaying of the boat, the environment was not conducive with training or any attempt to stay fit.

Louie found himself once again in the company of thieves as the athletes looted the cruise ship's stores of towels, ashtrays, and just about anything that was not bolted down; Louie was right at home. The ship had many other wonders for the depression era boy who had only eaten in a restaurant twice up until this point in his life. Between the three large meals a day and the poolside service, Louie had gained twelve pounds on his nine-day journey across the sea.

In Germany, the signs of war were everywhere. The buses had machine gun turrets. Military units drilled and the Luftwaffe put on aerial displays for the visitors. Germany welcomed the world to the Berlin games and made it very clear that they no longer felt constrained by the Treaty of Versailles. The soon-to-be-infamous swastika adorned every building and venue of the games and Louie took his pilfering to new heights when he stole a swastika flag from a government building.

The leaders of the 5000m field were all on the Finnish team. After just barely making the finals, Louie felt his chances at a medal were slight. His lengthy sojourn across the Atlantic had done a number on his conditioning. In the final race he got boxed in for most of the preliminary laps; by the time he decided to make his kick, the Finnish champ Gunner Hockert had already won. However, Louie's last lap was run in 0:56 — over ten seconds better than the pace set by Lehtinen when he posted the record time in the 1932 Olympics.

Louie became known as "the boy with the fast finish" and even Adolf Hitler wanted to shake his hand. Louie received a hero's welcome when he arrived back in Torrance and was paraded through the streets in a flatbed truck.

Into War

As the world was descending into chaos, Louie was living the life of a college track star at the University of Southern California and was determined to break the four minute mile. At the 1938 NCAA championships Louis was convinced he was ready to break that mark but runners had been instructed to stop Zamperini. Louie was boxed in and severely injured by the other runners. Running across the tape in first place, Louie had been badly cut and a rib had been cracked, but his time of 4:08.3 would stand as the NCAA record for the next fifteen years.

With war an ever present danger, Louie voluntarily joined the Air Corp to avoid being drafted into the Army. He washed out of his training because he did not like flying, but because he had not read his discharge papers, he was back in the Air Force a few months later when he was drafted. He began training at Ellington Field as a bombardier and became one of the best in his squadron.

While Louie was in Texas, the Japanese decided to force America's hand and draw her into war. As bombs rained down on Pearl Harbour, Zamperini and many of the other servicemen stationed on the mainland had no idea that their peacetime duty was about to end. Louie was in a theater when, without warning, the lights went up and all the servicemen were ordered back to base.

Part Two

The Flying Coffin

The attack on Pearl Harbour had been a terrible shock to the American people. The threat of a Japanese attack seemed very real to the majority of Americans, even though they were many miles from Hawaii. Fiorella La Guardia, the Civil Defence Minister, drove through the streets of Washington D.C. with sirens blaring, yelling "calm" into a loudspeaker.

Everyone remembers Pearl Harbour, but few people know about the many air raids and invasions that the Japanese were responsible for that week. The Pacific Ocean was thrust into war. Wake Atoll, a tiny piece of coral in the mid-pacific that was home to one airstrip and about 500 American servicemen, was one of the strategic targets the Japanese claimed in this period.

On August 19, 1942, Louie is in Torrance for one last visit before he heads off to war. His brother Pete is now a Chief Petty Officer in the Navy and both men are stationed in the Pacific Theatre.

Louie was assigned to the 372nd squadron and travels by train to his next air training center in Ephrata, Washington, a dried up lake bed that swirls with dust. This is where Louis meets Russell Allen Phillips for the first time. Louie and his pilot "Phillips" are inseparable. Phillips was a Methodist Minister's son and a natural on the stick of a plane. The young pilot spent a great deal of time writing to his high school sweetheart Cecile Perry and intended to marry her after he returned from the war.

The men of the 372nd are assigned a B-24 bomber that they name *Superman*. The crew was not excited about flying in a plane model that had been dubbed "the flying coffin."

"This Is It, Boys"

In November of 1942, *Superman* and the crew landed in Hickam Air Field on Oahu. The island was still recovering from the damage of the Japanese raid. The men, ready for action, were disappointed to find that the posting at Oahu was just more lectures, more training.

Hickam is where the boys of the 372nd had their first run-in with the Lieutenant in charge of flight schedules. The B-24's were unpredictable at best, and when one engine blew, the plane was nearly impossible to control. When one of *Superman's* engines went down, Phillips brought the plane down. The Lieutenant tried to order the men back into the air, but he backed off when the men invited him to make the trip with them.

It is on Oahu that co-pilot Charleton Hugh Cuppernell joined the crew. When they weren't in training the men spent their time on sea search missions, flying over the vast stretches of the Pacific looking for the enemy. The airman's workload was one day off, one day on, and the boys spent their alternate days searching for fun on the island. Louie and Phil loved to hang out at the officers' club, and at P. Y. Chong's a great steakhouse. Louie ran the airstrip on his days off, and tried to keep his body physically fit, since his Olympic dreams were still alive.

The first action *Superman* saw was in the raid on Wake, led by Colonel Matheny; the American planes took few casualties, and the assault was considered to be the first victory for the Allies in the Pacific Theater. The men of the 372nd almost missed the celebration as their bomb bay doors did not shut after the payload is released; they barely have enough fuel to make it home.

"Only the Laundry Knew How Scared I Was"

Major Jonathan Coxwell, George Moznette, and James Carringer, all friends of Phillips and Louie, took off from a beachside airstrip on Kauai on January 8, 1943. They were taking part in a three plane training mission. The other two planes returned. Crashes were all too common. In a two year period, 400 AAF crews were lost just flying to their postings in the Pacific Islands.

Phil was considered to be among the best pilots in their bomber group. Often brash and daring, the preacher's son never refused a dare. Flying into the heart of a storm to prove a point to his co-pilot Cuppernell, Phil lost control of the plane and the crew, tossed and disoriented, was only saved when radioman Harry Brooks located a signal from Hawaii and guided Phil out of the storm.

While all of the crewmen worried about the risks of aerial combat, Phil had the additional burden of being the pilot and knowing that if he made a mistake there were eight other men who would have to pay for it. Phil carried a bracelet that Cecy (his high school sweetheart) had given him, and a silver dollar as good luck charms.

Five Hundred and Ninety-four Holes

The *Superman* crew is sent on a bombing mission over Makin in the Gilbert Island chain. To the delight of his crewmates, Louie drops 3000lbs of explosives on some enemy outhouses. The crew survives the ordeal relatively unscathed and on April 18, 1943 they find themselves leading a bombing mission to the phosphate rich island of Nauru.

The bomber crews had been practicing bombing runs below 10,000ft since they started their training. These dangerous missions dramatically increased the effectiveness of anti-aircraft guns. The raid of Nauru is the first time that Phil and Louie get to implement this training and none of the airmen are looking forward to this mission.

The planes make it to Nauru and are able to drop their loads, but as soon as they have deployed their explosives, they are engulfed in a cloud of Zeroes. The much faster dogfighters rip through the bombers' formations causing chaos and ripping the planes apart. The gunners fire desperately at the agile Zeroes but they are moving fast and they have numbers. Stanley Pillsbury the waist gunner with shrapnel embedded into his leg, some that will remain there for the rest of his life, waits patiently for his shot. As Super Man pulled away from the island three Zeroes had followed. As Pillsbury shot down the last of the enemy planes he finally succumbed to the pain.

As Phil and the co-pilot Cuppernell land the badly damaged plane, Louie is ready with parachutes to slow the B-24 as the hydraulic fluid has been leaking since they left Nauru. The crew land on the island of Funafuti with one dead and 3 injured. By the ground crew's final count, *Superman* had 594 holes and would not fly another mission.

The Stinking Six

The same night as they lay asleep on Funafuti, the air raid sirens start to blare, Louis and Phil run for cover on the tiny island as six Japanese bombers make successive runs against the defenceless post. Stanley Pillsbury is helped to a concrete bunker with the rest of the casualties as the planes rip apart the island.

On the fourth pass, the bombers hit American planes that had been prepared to raid the Japanese stronghold on Tarawa that morning. The explosions shook the island. While many planes were damaged in the raid, *Superman*, a plane that was a total loss anyway, made it through the night unscathed. It was a different story for the tent that Louie and Phil had been sharing that night: when the two men returned to the tent that morning there was a smouldering crater in its place.

The Super Man crew, minus the four casualties and the plane, flew a different B-24 back to Hawaii. They were transferred to the 42nd Squadron of the 11th Bomb Group and stationed at Oahu. The men have plenty of time on their hands as they wait to be assigned to a new plane. Louis and Phil in their travels around Hawaii find fake air bases setup to fool Japanese reconnaissance and enjoy the beaches.

This period is also where they meet Francis McNamara,or "Mac," a tail gunner who had yet to see any action and was assigned to their crew. Mac loved sweets, and eating in general. The men also met "the Green Hornet," an old B-24 that had seen too much action and that had been cannibalized several times to keep other planes running.

"Nobody's Going to Live Through This"

On Oahu, Louie was in the best shape of his life. With Jeeps pacing him, Louie had worked his mile time down around the 4 minute mark. War or no war, Louie was on track for the next Olympics whenever they might occur.

The crew's down time was ended abruptly when a Lieutenant stopped their Jeep as they were headed onto the airfield. The boys had had a run in with this officer before when he had tried to make the crew go through a training run in a plane that only had three operational engines. Louie agreed to do the training run if the Lieutenant came along and the argument was ended. This time the mission was a search and rescue, Clarence Corpening and crew had not landed on Canton that morning, and the only plane that was available for the mission was "The Green Hornet."

The Daisy Mae, a B-24 piloted by Joe Deasy, took off with "The Green Hornet" and they flew side-by-side for the first 200 miles but they could not keep pace and eventually the planes parted company. When they reached the search zone, the co-pilot Cuppernell took the controls, a standard practice which allowed co-pilots to gain the hours they needed to get promoted. As they searched, engine number 1 died. There was a great deal of confusion as the engineer came to thread the engine. The power was cut to the wrong engine and suddenly only the right side of the plane had power.

There was not even a way to get the plane level before they reached the water and the crew braced itself for impact. The engineer had the worst job of all, as the raft had to be released from the plane as close as possible to the water, he had to wait until the last minute to pull the release cord or the raft would be miles away and completely useless to the survivors.

The impact of the crash wedged Louie under the waist gun mount and he found himself wrapped in wires. Louie remembers everything going dark and believes that he passed out during this time, and yet he woke, free from the entanglement, and swam to the surface.

PART III

Downed

The ocean's surface was a mixture of fuel, oil, and blood as Louie scanned the water for the rafts. The rubber vessels were moving through the currents and swimming after them would be a daunting task. Louie was able to catch the long cords that were attached to both rafts and then paddled over to the other survivors. Phil was bleeding profusely from his head and Louie tied a shirt around the injury and hoped for the best. The loss of blood severely weakened Phil and he lay in a semi-conscious state during the first few weeks of their journey. Mac was not injured physically, but it was clear from the panic stricken expression that he had been damaged in the crash. The three men were now securely in the rafts that would be their home for the next few months.

The sharks appear immediately and start their constant vigil. The sharks begin to make their presence felt by rubbing their backs along the undersides of the rafts. Batting at the sharks with oars becomes a daily activity.

As the men survey their supplies they realise that the rafts are not fully stocked. The raft did contain ration-D bars, a bitter chocolate designed to replace their daily caloric intake. As it is an older model raft, the men do not have a mast and sail; they are literally drifting through the middle of the pacific.

Missing At Sea

The next morning, the search and rescue mission begins. The planes are still looking for the original lost plane, which as it turns out went down almost immediately after take-off, and now for one of the rescue planes. This was life in the Air Force in World War Two, people went missing, and the men developed a cool detachment.

Louie wakes that morning to see the chocolate is gone and Mac is feeling guilty. Now they have no food, and water supplies that will run out on day 4. As the first day passes, the castaways are passed over by a rescue plane. While the plane does not see them, it does alert the men to the fact that they are drifting into enemy waters.

On June 4 1943, the official telegrams arrived notifying the families of the airmen on board the "Green Hornet" that their sons are missing at sea. The media in California was already running with the story of the Olympic miler lost at sea.

Thirst

The men are laying exposed to the elements as they drift along near the equator with no water. They begin to break out in sores, from a mixture of dehydration and salt burns. The men busy themselves whacking sharks. After three days of this, the rains come and they spread out and try to absorb as much water as they can. Louie, after several unsuccessful attempts to gather water, starts to pool water in his mouth and spit it into canteens.

Mistaking the still forms for dead, an Albatross lands on the raft. Louie kills the bird, and the men attempt to eat it raw. They elect to use the bird as bait and the tiny pilot fish they eventually catch are the first solid food that Phil and Louie have had since the crash. The men were aware of Samuel Coleridge's poem, but they needed to survive.

To pass the time the men sing hymns and shared stories. One of their favourite past times was describing recipes and meals that they had eaten. It did not matter how the conversation started, it always came back to food. One other topic of conversation was of men on rafts, like World War One ace Eddie Rickenbacher, who had spent 21 days in a rubber raft.

Sharks and Bullets

The men hear a plane's engine and begin to discuss if it is even worth their time to try and signal the plane. After they signal it the plane starts to head towards them and the men are overjoyed. When the plane comes within 200ft, it opens fire. The plane was Japanese.

The men were forced to take cover under the boats. After the plane passed, they got back in, but when it circled back, Phil and Mac decided just to curl up and hope for the best. Louie jumped into the water. The bullets were coming from above, but Louie had bigger problems with fins. As he waited for the plane to pass, the sharks were charging Louie and he had to punch them repeatedly in the snout.

Back on the rafts, the bullets had put holes all through the rubber rafts. The second raft was completely destroyed and now three men would be sharing one sinking raft. The men took turns, patching holes, pumping air, and whacking sharks. The deflating raft was inspiring the sharks to try harder to get at the men.

Singing in the Clouds

The sharks become extremely aggressive. As Louie leans his hand into the water, he is surprised by a shark springing out at him. Louie is saved by Mac. Mac and Louie, oars in hand, fight of the sharks and the act seems to bring the despondent Mac back around. He had been locked in a mix of shock and depression since the day that they had crashed.

This fight with the sharks enraged Louie. It was alright for them to attack when he went into the water but this had gone too far. Phil and Louie devise a plan to kill a shark as retribution. They realise that they need a small shark, and to get the tail out of the water, in order to stand a chance of getting a shark. The men manage to kill and eat two sharks during their voyage.

On the 33rd day, Francis McNamara dies. While the other two had managed to buoy their spirits, Mac had been sure he was going to die from the first day. His help fighting the sharks and his work when the rafts were sinking had completely redeemed Mac in the minds of his raft-mates. After the war when Phil and Louie were asked about their experience they left out the chocolate incident.

On the 40th day, the ocean was very peaceful and Louie could hear the most beautiful music emanating from a cloud. He claimed that he could make out 21 human figures in the cloud. The music would come back to Louie from time to time. Phil did not see it, but Louie refused to believe it was a hallucination. Six days later the men saw an even more spectacular sight: land!

Typhoon

The weather takes a turn for the worse, but the men realise that they are approaching a group of islands. They are also well aware that they are in enemy territory so they hold back, waiting for nightfall to find a safe place to land. When they finally make their approach they are spotted by a boat. They are blindfolded and beaten before being taken to an infirmary.

When the plane first went down, Phil and Louie weighed 150lbs and 155lbs respectively; after 47 days at sea, they are 80lbs and 87lbs. The men are fed a gigantic meal to try and recuperate some weight and then they are brought before a group of officers. The men had travelled over 2,000 miles to the Marshall Island chain.

During this stay the men are fed very well and get to sleep in beds, but they are told that their next stop will not be this pleasant. Kwajalein Island, A.K.A. "Execution Island" was a far cry from the hospital.

July 16, they arrive at Kwajalein and Louie is greeted with a kick to the face. He is thrown in a small wooden cell with nine names carved into the wall. When Louie inquiries about the men he finds out that these marines were all executed. At the age of 85, Louie would return to try and find the bodies of these men. Louie added his name to the list.

Part IV

A Dead Body Breathing

Louis had not had enough time at the hospital to regain the weight he had lost. The three golf ball sized portions of rice Louie was given every day on Kwajalein were not enough to try and recover. The food was just thrown into the cell and Louie was forced to pick rice off the gravel floor. He had to try and get by on two swallows of water a day, while at the same time dealing with explosive diarrhea.

Phil and Louie were in separate cells and could only talk when the guards were away. The guards were always making threatening gestures at the prisoners and things got worse if the guards were working in pairs, as they would beat the prisoners harder to impress each other with their love for the emperor.

Phil and Louie find out that they have been sent to this death camp so that the Japanese can extract information about the B-24 bombers and the Norden Bombsight. Louie had not even been allowed to show pictures of the sights to his family so he was sure he could not give away this information to the enemy. Phil and Louie worked on crafting believable lies and even gave the Japanese the locations of the fake airfields (although they left out the fake part) they had found while exploring Hawaii. By August 23, 1943 the men are being shipped from what they thought would be their final resting place to Yokohama, Japan.

Two Hundred Silent Men

After a three week journey, made a little better by a bottle of pilfered sake, the airmen are blindfolded and taken to Ofuna. This secret camp was a holding center for "unarmed combatants" and did not grant its inhabitants the rights that they might have been entitled to as prisoners. The inmates at this location were of a high profile nature and it was thought that they could be persuaded into helping the Japanese cause.

The first interrogator Louie met was his old college friend Jimmie Sasaki. The two men reminisced about the good old days and Louie waited for a grilling that would never come. Each interview with Sasaki followed the same format as the first.

Ofuna had many rules designed to give the guards reasons to beat and torture the inmates. Talking was forbidden, but most of the infractions were the result of the guards yelling Japanese commands at their English-speaking charges. One of their favourite punishments was the "Ofuna Crouch." A prisoner would stand with his knees bent half-way and his arms stretched above his head. The position would be held for as long as it was ordered and any faltering resulted in a beating.

Prisoners of war hoped for an end to the war, but Allied success was not a good thing for those in prison camps. The official Japanese policy was to kill all prisoners of war if the base or territory was going to be taken. The infamous "kill-all" rule was an ominous presence in the minds of the prisoners.

Farting for Hirohito

Every morning the men of Ofuna were forced to bow to the flag and salute the Emperor and every night the men stored up their gas to let one blast for Hirohito. This was just one of the many little acts of rebellion that allowed these men who had been stripped of their rights to try and maintain their dignity. Louie, against camp policy, kept a diary. William Harris, a marine with a photographic memory, made maps from glimpses at Japanese newspapers.

The men engaged in thievery on a large scale in the camp, to try and compensate for the lack of decent food, and as a way to strike back at their enemies. Newspapers were a hot commodity, men used them to keep up with the war and most prisoners had dysentery. Harris was one of the few captives that spoke Japanese; he even created his own phrase book to help him if he ever found a way to escape.

Fred Garrett, a B-24 pilot from California, sought Louie out when he arrived in camp. The pilot had his leg amputated by the Japanese because of a broken ankle. As he lay on Kwajalein trying to recover he saw names carved on the wall. The guards informed Fred that only Louis Zamperini was alive and Fred found hope in this. The two men quickly became friends.

In March, Phil and Louie are finally separated. Phil was sent to Ashio, a POW camp where men are forced to mine copper, but he is told that he can write home. His letter is found in the garbage by another POW. Phil decides he will deliver it in person.

Belief

The families of the "Green Hornet" crash are not willing to give up on their boys. They form support group and keep in close contact through letters. Louise even writes to General Hale to ask him to continue the search. The General refuses but the mothers and families refuse to give up.

In 1944, when Kwajalein was taken by the Allies, records of two downed airmen surface and a board with Louie's name carved into it are recovered, but the families are not notified.

Cecy, stricken with grief, tries anything to find out the truth about Phil's wreck. She moves to Washington D.C. just to try and learn the truth. She even consults a psychic. Cecy is not ready to give up on her fiancé.

Plots Afoot

Hearing planes take-off near the camp, Louie and Frank Tinker, a B-24 pilot, start to plot their escape. Bill Harris starts to plan out their route from his map collection. The men are all quite a bit taller than the average Japanese soldier so they realise that they will have to travel at night.

Louis takes a job as a camp barber as the guards will pay one rice ball per shave and he needs the extra food. While the prisoners were stealing from the guards they felt pushed to it by the guards and camp personnel who took the food intended for the prisoners for themselves. The cook was making a killing on the black market with the fresh food and the prisoners were forced to eat maggoty, lice-ridden food.

The plan to escape was foiled one day when the maps were discovered in Harris's possession. The inmates had to watch from an Ofuna Crouch position for 45 minutes while the guards laid a beating on Bill. On September 30th, 1944, the co-conspirators Louie and Frank are finally released from Ofuna to what they think might be a better life in an actual POW camp.

Monster

The prisoners are sent to a man-made island in Tokyo Bay to Omori. The camp had been a very easy going camp. As far as prison camps go, the men were treated with respect and the rules were loosely enforced. Everything changed when Corporal Mutsuhiro Watanabe was assigned to this posting. Born to a wealthy family, this French literature major assumed he would be an officer when he joined the cause. His position as an enlisted man was made even more undesirable by the fact that he was assigned to a prison camp and not to combat.

Watanabe realised that by being unpredictably and unmercifully cruel he could command the same type of respect that he desired. As a result of his viciousness, Watanabe "the Bird" was put in charge of discipline and the once docile Omori became known as a punishment camp. As the Bird walked out to greet the new prisoner this was Louie's first encounter with the man who would haunt his dreams years after he left Japan.

Louis was the just the sort of man the Bird liked to attack. The Olympic miler was strong-willed, successful, and unlike Watanabe, he was an officer. Watanabe would seek Louie out and beat him on an almost daily basis from this moment forward.

Hunted

Even his nickname was inspired by fear: Watanabe was called "the Bird" because it was a safe name that would not get anyone beaten if overheard. The Bird commanded fear and respect. His office was at the end of the main road in the camp. All of the barracks lined this road.

Prisoners leaving their barracks had to salute the Bird or at least his office or suffer through a beating. Watanabe would lie in wait with a club in hand ready to smack any inmate who did not salute his picture window.

In direct violation of the Geneva Convention, Watanabe forced Officers to work, although he did not send them out to work in the factories like enlisted men, he had the officers repair equipment for the Japanese Military. The officers could now engage in the guerrilla war that was being waged by the enlisted men.

Forced to work in Japanese factories and mines, the enlisted men were constantly pushing the boundaries in an attempt to sabotage the enemy. On the loading docks men mislabelled, redirected, and damaged military goods. Sinking barges, derailing trains, and pilfering goods were actions committed in the name of patriotism.

Louie spent his days trying to avoid the Bird. Watanabe wanted to make Louie look him in the eyes and submit to his authority, he wanted to see the vengeful fire burn out in the Olympian's eyes. As Louie faced the fists, kendo sticks, and clubs, he starred at the ground seething with rage.

B-29

Of all the horrible things the inmates of Omori were forced to eat, the protein allotment was probably the most questionable. Every week a wheelbarrow was pushed across the bridge into Tokyo and a butcher dumped intestines and unrecognizable hunks of horse out for the prisoners to eat. This week, it was Louie's turn to push the cart, and as he walked through Tokyo, the bombardier could see the horrifying effects of his trade. Looking up at the buildings Louie could see the writing on the wal:l "B-*niju-ku*," or B-29, the super fortress, the machine that would eventually turn the course of the war.

The presence of the B-29s made the Bird even more hostile. Taking off his belt, Watanabe whipped Louie across his temple with the large brass buckle. Louie had promised himself he would not go down for the Bird, but he dropped to the ground bleeding from his head. The Bird got a napkin for Louie to hold against the gash and helped him back to his feet just so that Louie would be surprised when the buckle hit the same spot a minute later.

Another violation of the Geneva Convention was that prisoners were not allowed to send letters home. Louie's family still had no idea that he was alive and so when Radio Tokyo asked Louie to record a message to his family he agreed to do it. Louie tried to make the message sound positive so that the enemy would use it.

Lynn Moody, a friend of Louie's from USC, was working at the FCC's propaganda department when she heard Louie reading his message on Radio Tokyo. Lynn and several short wave operators sent word to the Zamperini family. The War Department would not confirm the reports, but they did not need to; Anthony and Louise knew it was their Louie.

The family continued to believe in Louie even after his trunk came home, his life insurance paid out, his death announcement made headlines, and even though they acquiesced to director Cecile B. DeMille's demand that they talk about Louie as if he were dead for a radio interview, they never gave up hope.

Madness

The broadcast had been a hit and the Radio Tokyo people wanted more. They approached Louie with another radio spot, but this time they had a script prepared. He would have to go on the radio and condemn the American Government for relaying untrustworthy information. In exchange Louie would live a very comfortable life working in the Propaganda Department far away from the Bird and eating food fit for human consumption. Despite the many benefits, Louie told the producers he would not read their statement. They threatened him with a punishment camp, but Louie figured anything would be better than Omori. In the end, Louie was returned to Omori and the Bird and the daily attacks resumed.

Friday November 24, 1944 the B-29s start their bombing of Tokyo as 111 planes descend on the capital. The speedy Zeroes are no match for the flying fortresses. As the fall continued, civilians started to camp around the prison to avoid the air raids. The Bird would refuse to let the prisoners take cover.

When Prince Yoshitomo Tokugawa found out about the Bird's behaviour he pushed to have the Bird removed from power. The victory was a hollow one as Watanabe was promoted to Sergeant and sent to another prison camp. For the men of Omori, it was a great day. The camp immediately reverted to its former relaxed atmosphere.

Falling Down

The Omori guards let the POWs write home and the Red Cross packages that had been confiscated by the Bird were distributed to the prisoners. Bill Harris, who had finally been released from Ofuna, was deathly ill and Louie gave his package to Bill in hopes that it would revive the marine.

The B-29s flew unopposed through the skies around Tokyo and the prisoners could sense that the war was coming to a close. This was even more worrisome, than it was comforting, as the invasion of Japan would surely mean their deaths. The "kill-all" rule was being implemented throughout the Pacific as the Japanese retreated.

Now that the Bird was gone Louie started to worry about the threat of being sent to a punishment camp. Fifteen names were called out and Louie and many of his friends were loaded onto a truck and taken to the rail yard. He was being transferred to Naoetsu. Travelling all day by truck, train, and then hiking uphill through the snow Louie was greeted by a familiar scream. His legs locked and he fell to the ground.

Enslaved

Naoetsu, one of the worst camps Imperial Japan had to offer, was home to 300 residents. The men shared their living space with the ashes of 60 slaughtered Australian soldiers. The men were still wearing the tropical garb that they had been captured in. Louie was also wearing the same muslin shirt he had been wearing and as the temperatures were so low he soon developed a cough and flu-like symptoms.

As Louie shivered through the winter, Jim Rafferty, America's best miler, won the first Louis S. Zamperini Invitational. As spring arrived, the officers were sent to work on the farms. This work was not as hard as what the enlisted men were doing and since they were working they were given full rations. Officers were normally given only half rations as they were not required to do manual labor.

As a B-29 passed over this remote location it seemed a sure sign of Allied dominance. The attacks had moved on from Tokyo and the Japanese could offer little resistance. This made the Bird, or as the Aussie's called him, "Whatabastard," even crazier, and in a fit of rage the sergeant sent the officers to work on the coal barges.

While hauling a load of coal from the barge to a rail car, Louie was elbowed by a guard and sent hurtling to the ground. Only managing to get one leg underneath him, and with the added weight of the coal, Louie felt his leg snap and pain surged from his ankle to his knee. Unable to work, Louie was cut to half rations. Louie needed more food to try and heal his leg, cough, and his ongoing battle with dysentery. He went to the Bird to beg for work. Louie was put in charge of the camp pig, but he was only allowed to use his hands to clean out the sty.

220 Punches

Watanabe called the camp to attention. A foreman's fish had been stolen and even though it had been returned, a punishment was given out. The thieves had confessed, but Watanabe called up a group of officers, which included Louis, and accused them of inciting the theft. Their punishment was a punch in the face from every other man in the camp. If the punch was not hard enough, Watanabe made the prisoner do it again.

The situation was deteriorating as the B-29s increased in frequency and numbers the Japanese became more frantic. Camps started making preparations for the "kill-all" rule and prisoners began to suspect every order and every action as the possible signal of the end. The prisoners were tipped off by a civilian camp worker on August 22nd. The half-starved, unarmed men tried to come up with a plan to save themselves from the vile end that awaited them.

The Boiling City

Louie again tried to find work and secure full rations that he needed as he attempted to recover. The Bird gave Louie a sickly goat and told him that their fates were tied: if the goat dies, you die. Watanabe started telling Louie that he will drown him tomorrow. The next day he would appear and beat Louie as usual, but always renewing the threat. A few days later, Louie finds himself in a group of men forced to do push-ups over the hole in the *benjos*, or outhouse. The men who couldn't do the push-ups were pushed face first into the excrement.

August 6, 1945, a pilot named Tibbets takes to the skies and drops "Little Boy" on Hiroshima. The Japanese start to ask the prisoners about this weapon that vaporized a city, but the POWs know just as much about it as the Japanese. Three days later, it happens again.

The Naked Stampede

Rumours start to circulate that the war is over. Phil, now at Rokuroshi prison camp, was worried as the commander had left and the guards were forcing the POWs to go on long hikes into the wilderness. Every hike the men started to think it might be their last. The prisoners around Japan were all waiting for the "kill-all" to be ordered.

At Naoetsu, the Bird had disappeared and the camp's real commander dons his military finest to address the POWs. He tells the men that the war is over and that he hopes they will all join in the fight against the USSR as the Soviets were starting to take Japanese territory. The men could hardly believe their ears and many were convinced it was a trick. The men were invited to head down to the river and wash up.

As they run naked into the water a dive bomber starts heading their way. The men are completely exposed, and have no way to defend themselves; luckily, the plane is American and in Morse code the words of the camp commander are confirmed. A pair of pants full of goodies is dropped to the men. Inside the pants, the men find an article about the bomb that vaporizes cities.

Cascades of Pink Peaches

The POWs start to party and celebrate the end of the war. B-29s start to drop food to the men, who have been told to hold tight until evacuation crews have arrived, and the men gorge themselves. The half-starved men can barely hold any food down, but they are too happy to care. The feelings of anger and resentment are swept away in waves of ecstatic joy. Nothing matters anymore: they have peace.

The B-29 drops bring with them a new peril as the pallets of food start crashing into buildings, fields, and people. The Bird's office at Omori is crushed by a pallet of goodies. Overcome with glad tidings the men even start to offer their bounty to the people living near the camps. The people of Japan were, in many cases, as bad off as the prisoners.

September 2, 1945 Japan officially surrendered. With his new found freedom Louie attempted to clean the shirt he has been wearing since he boarded the "Green Hornet" on Oahu. After waiting for two weeks for an evacuation crew the ranking POW at Naoetsu, Fitzgerald, demanded a train and enough cars to run his men to Yokohama, Japan's biggest port. Fitzgerald stayed behind with those too ill to travel and refused to leave any POW behind.

Mother's Day

The POWs were in charge of the train and it stopped at every town along the route so the men could grab anything that was not nailed down. Sake was number one on the list and then men drank through the long trip to the sea. The soldiers began to cheer as they passed the charred remains of the cities. The carnage was amazing, but to the POWs these terrible scenes had saved them from execution, or worse life in a camp.

When they reached Yokohama the men were blown away by the Red Cross nurses. They had not seen women in a long time, but they were sure these women were goddesses. Journalist Robert Trumbull walked around Yokohama looking for a big story, and when somebody said he should talk to Louis Zamperini, Trumbull only had one problem with that: Zamperini was dead. Louie's family had received confirmation of his POW status in the early stages of 1945, but they had been asked not to discuss it by the War Department so most people still believed the miler was dead.

Louie showed Trumbull what little he had left in his wallet. It did not help that Louie was still just a walking skeleton. Trumbull took down Louie's story and then Louie was on a plane to Okinawa. The 11th Bomb group was stationed at Okinawa and they were all surprised to see Louie. The men had drank his liquor, tradition if a man died was to drink the liquor from his footlocker before sending it home, and now he was walking amongst them. The Zamperinis received the first notifications about Louie's trip home, not from military sources, but through Trumbull's article.

Louie was allowed to stay on Okinawa and try to regain some weight before he went home. Although he really just wanted to party, the Olympic and war hero was just enjoying his freedom. Phil and Louie, along with many other POWs, had been promoted during their internment they were both Captains now.

Russell Allen Philips returned home October 16, 1945 and 4 weeks later, in his in-law's backyard, he married Cecy. Later that same year Louie returns to California. His brother Pete goes AWOL because he cannot wait to see Louie.

Part V

The Shimmering Girl

Louie gets back to the house on Gramercy in Torrance and he eats and tells stories. The family is glad to see that he is the same Louie. His sister puts on a recording that Lynn Moody had sent the family of the Radio Tokyo broadcast and it sends Louie into a panicked rage. As Louie tried to adjust himself to civilian life he could not escape the Bird. Watanabe haunted Louie's dreams.

Louie was not alone, as officials took statements from prisoners the accusations against Watanabe mounted. 250 affidavits were taken concerning his actions and when the lists of war criminals came out Watanabe's name was in the same category as the man who engineered Pearl Harbour. Watanabe goes into hiding.

Everyone wanted to hear his story and Louie Zamperini was forced to relive his horrors in rooms of strangers night after night. After 95 speeches and countless interviews, Louie's nerves were out of control and he started drinking to numb himself. As a celebrity now, Louie got to fire the starting gun at the Louis S. Zamperini Invitational in New York. Louie began to train for the 1948 London Olympics.

On R&R in Miami Louie spots a beautiful girl walking through the bar. The wealthy girl falls for the runner from the wrong side of the tracks. She promises to help Louie with his demons and promises her parents she will wait for the fall to marry the runner. Louie Zamperini and Cynthia Applewhite are married May 25, 1946.

Coming Undone

In late 1946 the newlyweds head to dinner with Phil and Cecy and Fred Garrett everyone is happily discussing their future plans when a plate with white rice is put in front of Fred and he flies into a rage. 85% of Pacific POWs suffered from Post-Traumatic Stress Disorder. The men struggle to rebuild the dignity that they had lost in the camps.

During their honeymoon Cynthia's presence keep the Bird at bay. He was lurking in the dreams and as soon as they got settled into their new apartment he was back brass belt buckle in hand tormenting his favourite inmate.

Louie was training hard and already running the mile in 4:18. The passion was gone, Louie was forcing himself to keep going, but the running no longer brought him peace. He set out to run a two-mile with Cynthia timing him. He could feel his coal hauling injury as soon as he started, but Louie pushed through. He posted a great time. His ankle had given out, Louie's training was over. Now there was nothing to distract the soldier from his drinking.

Louie had been allowed to keep his life insurance payout and he was living on a string of investments. Louie went partying every night, but Cynthia stayed home. No matter how much he drank, Louie could not escape the flash backs; a car backfired and Louie ended up on the floor of the bar, quivering. He was in California, but at any sound or sight could send him right back to Japan, right back to the Bird. Louis decides the only way to get past this is to head back to Japan and kill the Bird.

The Body on the Mountain

As the authorities are searching for Watanabe he has found a sympathetic farmer and is hiding in the mountains near Nagano under the name Saburo Ohta. Other guards are being sentenced to life in prison and even being put to death. The Bird took a huge risk by visiting his family as they were all under surveillance and Watanabe narrowly escapes being detected. When he returns to Nagano the farmer introduces Watanabe to a young girl. Watanabe and the girl leave the farmer's house and the former disciplinarian tries his hand at cowherd.

In the fall of 1946, two bodies are found on Mount Mitsumine and they are identified as Watanabe and his wife.

Twisted Ropes

Louie, unaware of these developments, was still formulating his plan to hunt down the Bird. He was losing money all over the place with careless investments. He was considering a career as a mercenary and there was a growing distance between the newlyweds. Cynthia pleaded with Louie to quit drinking and even went back to her parents but she was not ready to give up on Louie and soon returned.

The 1948 Olympics came and brought only pain as Louie could not run. His creditors were starting to crack down on him. His convertible was repossessed. Louis begins to blame God for his problems and forbids Cynthia from going to church.

Cynthia is pregnant with their first child when Louie has another dream about the Bird. In the dream he has wrestled the Bird to the ground and is choking him. When he wakes up he is strangling his wife. When his daughter is born Louie loves her dearly, but his drinking is out of control. Cynthia, worried for their safety, takes her daughter and leaves.

A Beckoning Whistle

Shizuka Watanabe had not been convinced that it was her son on the mountain side in 1946 and those feelings were confirmed when she saw him in Tokyo in 1948. The authorities kept a close watch on the family and the case had not been officially closed so Watanabe only came to Tokyo to have dinner with his mother. As he leaves he tells her that he will see her in two years.

In September of 1949 Billy Graham sets up a tent in Los Angeles and starts to preach the gospel. Cynthia was back in California to finalize the divorce when a neighbor convinces her to go and hear the word. Cynthia experiences a religious awakening and for weeks she hounds Louie to go and hear Graham. At his first sermon Louie is scared, confused, and angered. He storms out and is only dragged to a second sermon under the understanding that he can leave when he wants to.

At the second meeting Louie experiences his last flashback. He finds himself taken back to the day when the ocean stood still and he was overwhelmed by the beauty of God's creation and he had made a promise to serve God if he would only save him from that ordeal. As this realisation washed over Louie it felt like those life-giving rains from his days on the raft.

Day Break

In the fall of 1950 Louie heads back to Japan to Sugamo Prison. The worst guards, with the exception of the Bird, from Ofuna, Omori, Kwajalein, and Naoetsu were being held there. Louie wanted to know if the peace he had found in Christ could withstand the sight of these men who had tormented him. Louie asked about the Bird and the Colonel who was guiding Louie said that Watanabe had committed suicide. To Louie's amazement he was filled with compassion for his tormentor. The guards from the camps Louie had stayed were asked to come forward, the new born Christian could not contain himself and he ran to greet them.

Characters

Adolf Hitler, who probably gets a mention in every book about WWII, gets onto these pages for his role in the 1936 Olympics.

Mutsuhiro Watanbe alias "the Bird" was the sadistic disciplinarian who ran the prison camp. Born into a wealthy family and educated at the finest schools Watanbe believed he would be made an officer like his brother and brother-in-law. When he was made a Corporal something inside this French Literature major snapped and he became a volitile soldier. In November of 1943 he was sent to Omori prison camp and his ruthlessness earned him the position of "dsciplinary officer." Corporal Watanbe escaped capture and was never tried for his war crimes.

Kunichi James Sasaki was a college friend of Louie's who often travelled to Torrance and was later revealed to be a Japanese spy. Louie ran into his old friend when he was sent to Ofuna where Jimmie was a civilian consultant put in charge of interrogation. In the many interviews the two men held at Ofuna Jimmie never discussed military matters preferring instead to relive their days at USC.

Pete Zamperini was the eldest of the Zamperini children. Pete had been a role model and coach for his younger brother. Pete served in the Navy and returned from the war to coach high school track and football.

Russell Allen Phillips was the pilot of Zamperini's crew and the two men go through everything together, from training, to battle, to internment, and eventual freedom. The man they called "Phil" returned to his hometown, married his sweetheart Cecy, and taught High school science

The rest of Zamperini's crew: co-pilot Charleton Hugh Cuppernell, engineer and top-turret gunner Stanley Pillsbury, engineer Clarence Douglas, navigator Robert Mitchell, Radioman Frank Glassman, tail gunner Ray Lambert, and waist gunner Harry Brooks. The crews changed as the war moved on but this was the crew that saw battle at Nauru.

Bill Harris, the son of a General, met Louie at Ofuna and created his own Japanese-English translation guide from scraps of paper and cardboard. He translated news of the war from Japanese newspapers. A remarkable man, he stood 6'2" but those around him thought of him as a giant with estimates of his height being around 6'10". Harris survived the prison camps with Zamperini returns to serve with the Marine Corps in the Korean War and won the <u>Navy Cross</u>, but did not return.

Fred Garrett, a B-24 pilot from Burbank, CA, had his leg amputated because of a broken ankle, while being held at the Kwajalein detention center. He lay in his cell assured of his death when he noticed names on the wall. Asking the guards, Garrett found out that one man, Louis Zamperini, had survived. When the two men meet at Ofuna, Garrett tells Louie about how his name on the wall had given the young pilot the strength to carry on.

Key Terms

- The "greenhouse" was the glassed in section below the bomber where the bombardier sat.

- The Zero was the Japanese fighter plane that ruled the skies over the Pacific for the first half of the war. The speedy planes were designed for "dog fights" and could pick bombers to peices with machine gun fire.

- The <u>Geneva Convention</u> established the <u>Red Cross</u> and set down rules for the treatment of POWs. The Japanese signed the Treaty, but never ratified the decision, their treatment of POWs was completely out of line with the rules set down in Switzerland in 1864.

- Kwajalein was the first interrogation center Louie and Phil are taken to after they leave the infirmary. It was known as "Execution Island." The two men were subjected to constant beating and humiliation during this time. Submarine crews stopping on the island in the Marshall Islands would often beat the prisoners as a form of entertainment.

- The "Kill-all rule" was the English description of the Japanese policy of killing all POWs when their positions were under attack. 90+ American prisoners were killed when Wake Atoll was attacked in 1943.

- Ofuna was a secret holding center for high profile prisoners the men were considered "unarmed combatants" and not given the rights of POWs. At Ofuna a strict code of obedience was enforced. The men were only allowed to look at the ground and had to remain silent. The prisoners had to ask for provisions in Japanese this included water and permission to use the toilet. Prisoners were allotted 500 calories of moldy, rancid food a day while being forced to exercise.

- Omari POW camp was a slave labor camp like most Japanese camps. The men were forced to work in the shipyards, railyards, loading stations, and coalyards. Louie, as an officer, was exempt from this manual labor. The island was man-made and had a view of Tokyo. The Island was described as unworldly gray.

Major Themes

There are many themes running through Zamperini's life and consequently this story. Generally we reserve this term for works of fiction but I think this is an interesting way to approach this story.

Trials and tribulation of immigration to the United States.

Louis and his family have to deal with bigotry, poverty, and all with the added boundary of language. Anthony and Louise Zamperini spoke only Italian when they arrived in New York. The boys take to the streets as young boys and Hillenbrand points to their place as immigrants, as outsiders to explain the thievery and brawling.

Seeking diversions

Finding distractions was a big part of coping with the death, horror, and boredom of life as an airman. The bunker Louie lived in was wallpapered with pornography and the men were always heading to the Officer's club to meet women. Excessive drinking became the norm and Louie would have to battle the demons he had repressed before he could rejoin the civilian world.

The shortcomings of the B-24 Consolidated Liberator

The vast majority of airman deaths were completely unrelated to combat damage. Many planes were just lost or crashed on training runs. Only one plane out of every six was lost in combat. The planes had no steering on the ground and were very hard to control if an engine should die.

Running

Running is a big part of Louie's life even after the Olympics. He continued to train and claimed to be in the best shape of his life when he was stationed at Oahu just before his fateful flight. When the Japanese captors realised they had Louis Zamperini the track star in their camp they began racing him against local runners. The first race Louie was still too weak and he lost badly. The second he won and was beaten unconscious as a consequence. In his third race Louis was paid 2 balls of rice to throw the race and he was more than happy to oblige.

Dignity

Dignity, as an essential part of human life, is a central message that comes out of this story. Prisoners found strategies to preserve dignity in little acts rebellion and these acts were as important as food to the survival of the prisoners. When Louie wins the second race he knew he would be beaten, and yet the victory was worth the punishment.

Interesting Facts

- This book is full of amazing facts about Zamperini, the war, the planes, and the camps. Hillenbrand is a very thorough researcher and loves to tie facts into her anecdotal tales. The following list is just some food for thought derived from the questions I asked myself after reading this book.

- As a kid Zamperini read Zane Grey novels, there are over 80 published titles released by Grey between 1903 and 1940.

- During his College days Louie worked as an extra in Hollywood movies. At least one of these films starred Errol Flynn.

- The current NCAA record in the mile is 3:52.44, set by Syndey Maree, and 13:08.4 in the 5000m set by Henry Rono, neither athlete is a US citizen.

- The B-24 Liberator bomber was designed by David Davis of Consolidated Aircraft in 1938 after the company received an order from the US Air Corp for B-17s.

- More than 140,000 allied soldiers served as POWs in Japanese camps during WWII.

- Louis Zamperini gives some of the credit for his recovery and turn to spirituality to American Evangelist Billy Graham.

- The Billy Graham Evangelical Association has taken their message to 220 million people in over 200 countries.

- According to the Center for Disease Control (CDC) 80% of Americans living with Chronic Fatigue Syndrome are unaware of it.

Additional Sources

www.youtube.com/watch?v=I9O5yVzc0vQ

The fox news special report on Zamperini. There are a number of other videos about Zamperini that have also been uploaded to Youtube.

http://www.facebook.com/pages/Louis-Zamperini/103126083060897

Zamperini's facebook page.

http://www.mickmel.com/blog/201101/a-timeline-of-louis-zamperinis-journey/

A blog that has a detailed timelines of Zamperini's journey it was done after the author was inspired by reading the book.

http://www.americainwwii.com/stories/luckylouie.html

An article about Zamperini on a site about the American involvement in WWII

http://www.la84foundation.org/6oic/OralHistory/OHZamperini.pdf

A written transcript from an interview with Zamperini. The goal of the project was to tell the stories of California's best athletes.

http://www.keynotespeakers.com/zamperini/index.php

If you would like to book Louis for a speaking engagement.

http://www.louiszamperini.net

Seems to be the same page. But it is the official Louis Zamperini page.

http://athleteoutreach.com

A website that compiles inspirational stories from athletes (Zamperini is one of those stories).

http://www.runnersworld.com/article/0,7120,s6-243-297–13773-0,00.html

An article about Zamperini in this online magazine. I believe they are just trying to sell more shoes but it is an interesting read nonetheless.

http://www.teamusa.org

The official website of the United States Olympic Committee.

http://www.teamusa.org/news/article/28932

The direct link to their article on Zamperini.

http://www.usctrojans.com/sports/c-track/spec-rel/102611aaa.html

The article on the website of Zamperini's alma mater the University of Southern California about him receiving the 2012 NCAA inspiration award.

http://www.time.com/time/specials/packages/completelist/0,29569,2035319,00.html

Unbroken made Time's Top ten of everything in 2010 in the non-fiction book category.

http://www.mansell.com/pow-index.html

This site is dedicated to the memory of Roger Mansell and has compiled information on the POW's taken by the Japanese during WWII. Roger Mansell's book The Forgotten Men of Guam will be published in the fall of 2012 almost two full years after his death. The site contains some very interesting primary sources.

http://www.loc.gov/vets/

The Veterans History Project is a collection of oral histories collected by the American Folklife Center of the Library of Congress. There is a special section for the stories of American POW's from the Pacific theatre of WWII.

http://www.118trs.com/landing-page

Started By the grandson of Earl J. Davis, the site is dedicated to telling the stories of the 118th Tactical Reconnaissance Squadron in which Davis served. Some of the men ended up in camps that Louie was in.

Like then Share!

Click to share a free copy with your Facebook friends

(Don't worry, it won't auto share!)

About The Author

Brett Keith Davidson

Davidson received his BA from the University of Windsor and his MA from Carleton Universitity. He teaches history at Eldercollege in Windsor, Ontario and has published a biography of Charles G.D. Roberts. You can follow his blog at www.hubpages.com/bkeithdavidson.

About The Publisher

Hyperink is the easiest way for anyone to publish a beautiful, high-quality book.

We work closely with subject matter experts to create each book. We cover topics ranging from higher education to job recruiting, from Android apps marketing to barefoot running.

If you have interesting knowledge that people are willing to pay for, especially if you've already produced content on the topic, please <u>reach out</u> to us! There's no writing required and it's a unique opportunity to build your own brand and earn royalties.

Hyperink is based in SF and actively hiring people who want to shape publishing's future. <u>Email us</u> if you'd like to meet our team!

Note: If you're reading this book in print or on a device that's not web-enabled, **please email** <u>books@hyperinkpress.com</u> with the title of this book in the subject line. We'll send you a PDF copy, so you can access all of the great content we've included as clickable links.

READERS WHO ENJOYED THIS BOOK ALSO ENJOYED!

George Beahm's I, Steve: Steve Jobs In His Own Words

$2.99

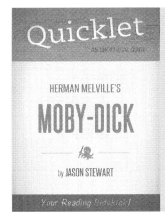

Herman Melville's Moby-Dick

$2.99

The JFK Assassination

$1.99